Given to the Kindergarten classroom
to celebrate being Star of the Week
by
Jordan Dohanyos, son of Franklin Joseph Dohanyos
November 12, 2001

Joseph's Story

Joseph's Story

Story by Patricia A. Pingry

Paintings by George Hinke

CandyCane Press

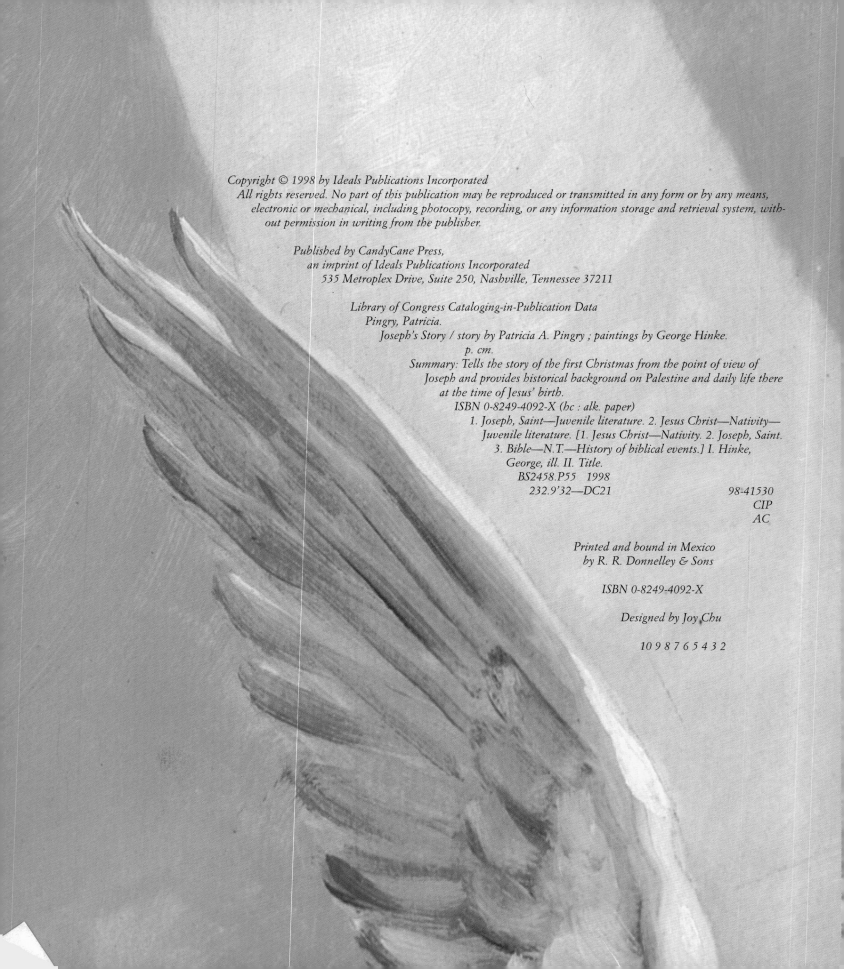

Copyright © 1998 by Ideals Publications Incorporated
All rights reserved. No part of this publication may be reproduced or transmitted in any form or by any means, electronic or mechanical, including photocopy, recording, or any information storage and retrieval system, without permission in writing from the publisher.

Published by CandyCane Press,
an imprint of Ideals Publications Incorporated
535 Metroplex Drive, Suite 250, Nashville, Tennessee 37211

Library of Congress Cataloging-in-Publication Data
Pingry, Patricia.
    Joseph's Story / story by Patricia A. Pingry ; paintings by George Hinke.
        p. cm.
    Summary: Tells the story of the first Christmas from the point of view of Joseph and provides historical background on Palestine and daily life there at the time of Jesus' birth.
    ISBN 0-8249-4092-X (hc : alk. paper)
    1. Joseph, Saint—Juvenile literature. 2. Jesus Christ—Nativity—Juvenile literature. [1. Jesus Christ—Nativity. 2. Joseph, Saint. 3. Bible—N.T.—History of biblical events.] I. Hinke, George, ill. II. Title.
    BS2458.P55 1998
    232.9'32—DC21   98-41530
                                                                                    CIP
                                                                                    AC

Printed and bound in Mexico
by R. R. Donnelley & Sons

ISBN 0-8249-4092-X

Designed by Joy Chu

10 9 8 7 6 5 4 3 2

An Historical Note

JOSEPH'S STORY takes place over two thousand years ago in the country of Israel, a region of about eight thousand square miles on the eastern edge of the Roman Empire. Joseph and his wife, Mary, lived in Nazareth in the province of Galilee. An angel named Gabriel had come to Mary and announced that she would have a Son. The angel said, "You will call him JESUS. He will be great and will be called the Son of the Highest: and he will rule his people for ever. He will be called the Son of God."

But one day a Roman soldier announced the news that there was to be a census and each family was to go to their ancestral city to be counted. Joseph's ancestor was King David, who was from the small village of Bethlehem in the province of Judea.

Bethlehem was an ancient city. One of the most tender love stories of all time, the courtship of Ruth and Boaz (Ruth 2–4), took place in the fields around Bethlehem. The prophet Samuel came to the hills around Bethlehem to find the great-grandson of Ruth and Boaz, a shepherd boy named David, whom Samuel would anoint as the first King of Israel. The prophet Isaiah had foretold, "But thou, Bethlehem Ephratah, out of thee shall he come forth unto me that is to be ruler in Israel...." (Micah 5:2). That ruler would be the long-awaited Messiah, and His name was Jesus, the descendant of Ruth and of King David. The caretaker of Baby Jesus was Joseph, who provided the earthly needs for the Baby and His mother. On the following pages is *JOSEPH'S STORY*.

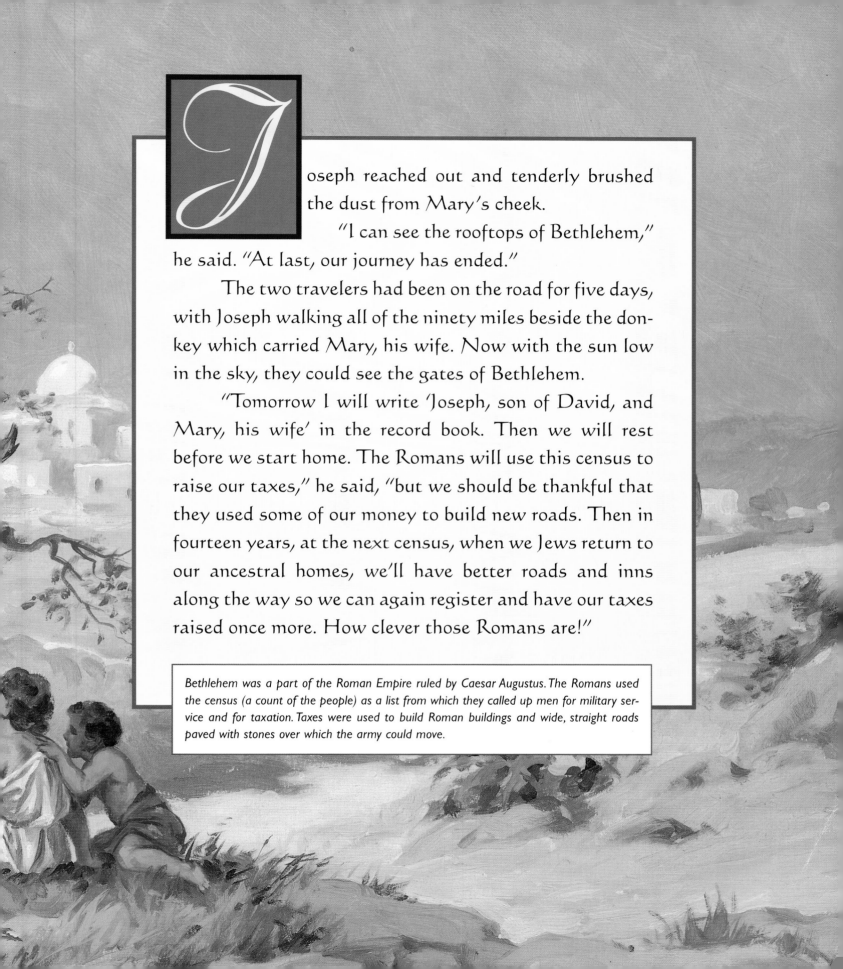

oseph reached out and tenderly brushed the dust from Mary's cheek.

"I can see the rooftops of Bethlehem," he said. "At last, our journey has ended."

The two travelers had been on the road for five days, with Joseph walking all of the ninety miles beside the donkey which carried Mary, his wife. Now with the sun low in the sky, they could see the gates of Bethlehem.

"Tomorrow I will write 'Joseph, son of David, and Mary, his wife' in the record book. Then we will rest before we start home. The Romans will use this census to raise our taxes," he said, "but we should be thankful that they used some of our money to build new roads. Then in fourteen years, at the next census, when we Jews return to our ancestral homes, we'll have better roads and inns along the way so we can again register and have our taxes raised once more. How clever those Romans are!"

Bethlehem was a part of the Roman Empire ruled by Caesar Augustus. The Romans used the census (a count of the people) as a list from which they called up men for military service and for taxation. Taxes were used to build Roman buildings and wide, straight roads paved with stones over which the army could move.

They stopped before an inn, and Joseph went inside to ask about a room for the night.

When he came back, he told Mary, "There are no rooms left here or anywhere else tonight. All Judea seems to be in Bethlehem, but the innkeeper's kind wife gave us the stable. You will be out of this cold wind, and I can find clean straw for a bed."

Joseph helped Mary slide off the donkey and into the stable. He then went to find some water with which to wash. He knew the donkey would find some grass to eat and Mary would set about to prepare the bread. They would also have some grapes and fresh figs that Joseph had purchased on the road.

After eating, Joseph made a soft bed beside the cow and the donkey. Mary was soon asleep, but Joseph stayed awake a long time. He thought about buying food for the next day. He thought about the long trip back home. He planned his spending so as to have enough coins for lodging and food. And he thought about the Child that was coming.

On their trip, Mary and Joseph probably carried water in a goatskin bag and food in a straw basket. There was no oven along the way, but Jewish women often dug a small hole in the ground, lighted a fire in the hole, placed smooth stones on top of the fire, then baked their bread on top of the hot stones.

ometime in the middle of the night, Mary shook Joseph awake. "Please go quickly and ask the innkeeper's wife to come and help. The Child will be born soon."

Joseph ran to the inn to get help. While the innkeeper's wife helped deliver the child, Joseph carried fresh water to the stable door and then waited outside. The stars seemed extremely bright. Looking up, Joseph saw stars and planets, some were so close together that they appeared to be one huge star.

"That bright star seems to hover right over our stable," Joseph thought.

After what seemed to be a very long time, the innkeeper's wife came out of the stable to tell Joseph that they had a baby boy. The Child and Mary were sleeping.

Joseph looked down at the sleeping Baby and said, "We will call you Emmanuel—Jesus—just as the angel from God told us to do."

Joseph remembered his visit from the angel and

how frightened he had been until the angel said that he had come with a message from God: Mary would have God's Son and His name would be Jesus.

But the angel had not told Joseph that the Child would be born in Bethlehem. The angel did not say there would be no rooms left at the inn or that Joseph's beloved Mary would have to sleep on a bed of straw.

"Dear Mary," Joseph whispered. "I am sorry that I could not have provided a proper bed for you. I am sorry that this Child must be placed in a manger where only a few hours before the cows ate their hay. We should wrap this blessed Babe in robes of silk, not in these strips of rags."

But Mary only stirred and placed her hand over Joseph's.

Joseph would not have stayed with Mary during childbirth; it was not the custom. After fetching water, Joseph would have waited outside. After newborns were washed, they were rubbed with salt, which was believed to prevent infection. Then the baby was wrapped in swaddling, strips of cloth that were not always new. These strips were wound tightly around the arms and legs to help them grow straight. Once a day, the strips were unwound and the baby was washed and wrapped up again.

Joseph lay down to sleep. He had just closed his eyes when he heard shouting. Peeking out the door, he saw a small crowd coming down the road.

"Where is He, the blessed holy Baby?"

"Is this the manger where our Savior lies?"

"We have followed His star!"

Joseph knew they were seeking Jesus. But how did they know? The Boy was barely a few hours old!

When Joseph stepped out into the cold night air, he saw several men whom, by their ragged clothes and barnyard smell, he knew to be shepherds. Their long staffs only confirmed this fact.

"Shhhh . . . , quiet, please. He is here," Joseph said. "But how did you know about this newborn Child?"

"The angels told us," said one of the shepherds. "We followed the star until it stood over this stable."

"See!" shouted one of the shepherds. "The star hangs over this manger."

Joseph looked up into the bright night sky. "The star does seem to hang over our stable," he thought.

"Please let us come in and see Him," spoke one of the younger shepherds. "We wish to worship Him."

"We'll tell you of the amazing things we have seen and heard this night," said another shepherd.

Shepherds in Israel didn't drive their flocks, they led them and lived so close to them that each sheep knew his shepherd's voice. The shepherd wore a camel-hair cloak and carried a rod and a sling for defense against wild animals and a six-foot staff for lifting the sheep out of danger.

One shepherd tugged at Joseph's sleeve, "I was asleep, huddled against the cold wind, and I awoke to a great noise! "

"The sky was open and we saw heaven!" shouted another.

"Yes, a hundred angels were in the sky!" shouted another shepherd. "They hovered over us. Singing!"

" 'Glory to God in the highest!' " practically all of the shepherds yelled at once.

"I was so frightened; I tried to hide under my sheep," spoke one of the young shepherds. "Then one angel came down and spoke directly to us."

"What did he say?" asked Joseph.

"He said," another shepherd interrupted, "that a Savior, which is Christ the Lord, had been born today!"

"In Bethlehem," said another, very loudly. "And lying in a manger!"

"So we came," offered another shepherd. "We knew that so many angels and so much noise and singing must have come from God."

"And . . ." whispered a very old shepherd, "we have waited all of our lives for the Savior promised by God."

In the Bible, some angels looked like men; others, seraphim and cherubim, had wings. The angel Gabriel told Mary that her Child would be God's Son. An angel appeared to Joseph three times: to tell him the Child's name would be Jesus, to go to Egypt, and that it was safe to go home. The angels that appeared to the shepherds numbered in the hundreds and may have included cherubim and seraphim. They were all "singing and glorifying God."

Joseph led the shepherds into the stable and showed them where Baby Jesus was now awake and lying in Mary's lap.

The shepherds fell to their knees, murmuring,

"Glory to God in the Highest . . ."

"Our Savior, Christ the Lord!"

"To actually see Him!"

"I never thought . . ."

"Praise God!"

"Peace on earth . . ."

Joseph knew the shepherds spoke the truth. This blessed holy Baby was indeed the long-awaited Messiah. That is what the angel meant when he told Joseph almost a year ago that the Child would be the Son of God.

"I wonder . . . ," mused Joseph under his breath, "Did God arrange those stars outside just to lead the shepherds here?" Joseph gazed in awe at the Child just born.

After the shepherds had gone, Joseph thought about what the Child needed: a real bed and clean clothes and a home. But first, Joseph would have to take Jesus and His mother on another long, hard trip—back to Nazareth.

Jesus was the Son of God, but Joseph took care of the Baby on earth. Jesus was the Messiah for whom the people had waited and of whom prophets had foretold, as did Isaiah, who wrote: "For unto us a child is born, unto us a son is given; and the government shall be upon his shoulder: and his name shall be called Wonderful, Counsellor, The mighty God, the everlasting Father, The Prince of Peace" (Isaiah 9:6).

Early the next morning, Joseph asked the innkeeper's wife to stay with Mary while he went into the city to write his name in the census book: "Joseph, son of David."

Now their business in Bethlehem was finished, but Mary would not be able to travel for several weeks. Each morning, Joseph counted out the coins he could afford to spend on food that day. Then he went to the inn to ask the innkeeper's wife to help Mary with Baby Jesus. Finally, he left to do his chores.

First he looked for other travelers who might need their wooden wagon wheels repaired. Joseph, being a good carpenter, could fix the broken wheels. Or he asked the men doing business at the city gates if they knew of anyone who needed a chair built, or perhaps a table.

Before he returned to Mary and Jesus, Joseph went to the bazaar and bought grain and grapes. Sometimes he found fresh figs, pomegranates, and tomatoes. He hauled water from the city well for washing. He brought hay for the donkey. He found fresh, clean straw for the manger and for the family's beds.

At night, Joseph was so tired that he fell asleep the moment he lay down.

Bethlehem was on a major trade route; everything could be bought at the marketplace. The coins used for money had the head of the Roman Emperor on one side. The coins that Joseph used probably bore the likeness of Caesar Augustus, the ruler of the Roman Empire at the time.

One night, Joseph heard more company coming up the path. When he went outside, he saw three camels lumbering toward the stable.

The camels stopped right in front of him, and their riders dismounted. They slowly walked toward Joseph.

"Is this where we will find the King of the Jews?" one of the men asked. "We have seen His star in the East and have come to worship Him."

Joseph had never seen such men. What marvelous clothes they wore! What grand saddles they had. They had rings and jewels on all of their fingers. They must be kings. They were certainly very rich.

"A Baby is here," Joseph answered. "Did you see angels also? Did they tell you about the Boy?"

"We have seen no angels," replied one of the kings. "We came from a land far to the east of here."

"For years we have studied the ancient writings," spoke up another king, "and we have looked to the sky for the promised sign."

"Finally, we saw the star! The star that means a King has been born in Judea," spoke the youngest king. "We followed this star for months, across the desert, along the trade routes, behind caravans and camels, all the long way from our home. We first went to Jerusalem, but the star led us here."

Little is known of the Magi except that they were "from the East." They might have come from Persia (modern Iran), or Babylon (modern Iraq), or from the desert of Arabia. No one knows why they followed the star, nor can anyone explain the star, but the Magi believed it meant a new king had been born. They naturally first sought him in Jerusalem, the capitol of Judea.

Suddenly Joseph felt the chill of fear. "You have been to Jerusalem?" he asked.

"Oh, yes," replied the tallest king. "We thought the King of the Jews would be there, in Judea's capital city."

"We were allowed an audience with King Herod, but Herod thought that he was King of the Jews," chuckled the shortest king. "Naturally he asked us to return after we had found the Child and tell him what we found."

"He is not to be trusted," piped up the youngest king. "We each had a dream warning us not to return to Jerusalem but to go home straight across the desert."

"We will not return to Herod," said the oldest, and perhaps the wisest, king. "But may we see the young King? We have traveled very far."

"Of course," answered Joseph. "We are pleased that you have come."

Tradition has given the Magi names, although the Bible does not. They are assumed to have been three and wealthy, because they brought three expensive gifts. Since they spoke directly with King Herod, they are also assumed to have been kings.

Joseph welcomed the kings into the stable to meet Mary and the Child. Each entered with a gift in hand.

The tallest king placed a jar in front of the manger. "This frankincense I give to You. Its sweet-smelling smoke brings with it a prayer of peace."

The youngest king came forward and placed a brass vase before the manger. "I offer You myrrh, the oil for the anointing of kings; and with it I give You my life."

The oldest king sat down a heavy chest. He was breathing very deeply. Slowly he opened the lid, and Joseph saw that it was filled with gold coins.

The king softly said, "You may soon have need of gold, my Lord."

"We thank you for all these gifts," said Joseph softly. "They are very fine gifts for this holy Child."

Before the manger, three kings in satin robes silently kneeled with heads bowed. Then, one by one, they slowly rose and slipped out into the night.

The gifts of the Magi are symbolic of the role Jesus was to play in man's life. Gold is rare and valuable; it might have been coins, a bowl, or a sculpture. Gold honored Jesus as King and could also have been practical, allowing the family the means to escape to Egypt. Frankincense, a gum from trees of southern Arabia and northern Somalia, was combined with other aromatic resins to make incense and burned in the Temple as an offering to God. Some people think that frankincense given to Jesus symbolized prayers. Myrrh is an aromatic resin from a tree native to southern Arabia and eastern Africa. Its oil was used in cosmetics and as a painkiller when mixed with wine. It was also used to anoint a body before burial. Myrrh symbolized suffering and indicated that Jesus was human and would die.

It was still dark the next morning when Joseph awoke. It was also very quiet. The three kings had ridden off on their long journey home. The shepherds were back with their sheep. It was now time for Joseph to pack up his family's things, strap their few possessions on the donkey, and help Mary and Jesus upon the donkey's back. It was time to leave Bethlehem.

"Mary," Joseph whispered to his still sleeping wife. "It is time to go."

"Are we going home today?" asked Mary.

"No," said Joseph. "We cannot go home yet. An angel came to me last night in a dream and told me that King Herod would try to hurt this Child. We must go far away until it is safe to return to Nazareth."

"Not go home?" Mary gasped.

"It will be all right," said Joseph, "I'll take care of you and Baby Jesus, and God will guide and protect us. Hurry now! We must be on our way."

King Herod the Great was the Jewish king of Judea but had to answer to Rome. His ten-year rule was marked by building: palaces and a Temple. He was mean; he had three of his own sons killed. After the Magi visited Herod, he was frightened of the new king. Since the Magi had seen the star two years earlier, Herod ordered every male child in Judea under two years of age be killed.

Joseph led his little family south and west. He and the donkey walked from sunup to sundown. Along the way, he bought fresh figs and tomatoes to eat; he found wells from which he drew water. The road was a caravan route, and each evening, Joseph found an inn where they could stay the night. Mary baked their bread and cared for Baby Jesus, and Joseph tenderly watched over them both.

After what seemed like a long time, they crossed into Egypt and stopped at a small village. Here Jesus grew. He smiled and laughed. He reached out and crawled. He learned to walk and to talk.

Joseph made yokes for oxen and sold them to the caravans that travelled through the village. Every morning Joseph prayed for God's help in caring for his family. Every night Joseph prayed that God would soon tell him that it was time to take his family home.

Joseph's journey to Egypt was probably west to the shores of the Mediterranean Sea, then along a well-traveled coastal road to Egypt, passing through the Sinai Peninsula. The Sinai is a wasteland of rocky mountains with high sand dunes along the shore. This is the wilderness where, centuries earlier, the Jews had wandered for forty years after their Exodus from Egypt.

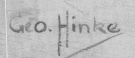

The little family lived in Egypt for several years until one night an angel came to Joseph in a dream. In the morning, Joseph awoke Mary.

"Mary, Mary," cried Joseph. "Today we start for home! The angel told me last night that King Herod is dead! It is safe to go back to Nazareth."

"Home!" cried Mary. "Oh, how I've missed my family!"

Joseph and Mary quickly packed up all of their belongings. He helped Mary and Jesus up on the donkey's back, and they started another journey. But this time, their faces were turned toward home.

Each night Joseph and Mary would plan the next day. Joseph talked to other travellers about what roads were safe and where he would find an oasis and water.

After many weeks, Joseph led them over the last hill, and there, standing on the next hill, was Nazareth. The fields on the surrounding hills were covered with fig and date palms, pomegranate trees and vineyards. They were green with wheat and barley.

"Ah, Joseph," Mary said, "how I love these beautiful hills and valleys. It's so wonderful to be home. Jesus will grow strong here."

"Yes," Joseph said, "and we have so much to tell: about His birth, about the shepherds, the kings, the angels. I'll teach Jesus how to be a carpenter. He will grow strong and wise, and we will have a blessed family."

On the return to Nazareth, Joseph led his family back across the deserts, but not through Judea, ruled by Herod's son Archelaus. Joseph followed the Mediterranean coastline. Nazareth was on a hill with a wide plain to the south and mountains in the other directions. It had enough rain and rich soil for growing fruits, grains, and vegetables. This would be Jesus' home for the next thirty years.

Afterword

Jesus grew to manhood in Nazareth. At about the age of thirty, He began His ministry. For the next three years, Jesus healed the sick, performed miracles, and taught the people about God.

One Sunday, Jesus rode into Jerusalem on a donkey. The people cheered and clapped and shouted "Hosanna!" But five days later, Jesus was crucified and buried in a tomb.

After Jesus had been in the tomb three days, an angel rolled away the stone at the door of the tomb and Jesus walked out. He was alive! His followers saw Him. They talked to Him. They ate with Him.

Then Jesus went up into Heaven to be with God, leaving His followers with the words, "And lo, I am with you alway, even unto the end of the world" (Matthew 28:20).

GALILEE

Nazareth ●

Sea of Galilee

Jordan River

JUDEA

Jerusalem ★

Bethlehem ●

Salt Sea

GREAT SEA
(MEDITERRANEAN SEA)

SINAI

EGYPT

Nile River

- - - - - Possible Route of the Journeys of Mary, Joseph, and Jesus

· · · · · · · Possible Route of the Journeys of the Magi